Samantha's Fun FM and Hearing Aid Book!

Samantha Brownlie

ISBN-13: 978-1466327177

Thanks and love to Mom, Dad and Sean

...And special thanks to Karen Ard

Hi. My name is Samantha. I am six years old. I love cats. I turned seven.

Hi,

My NAME IS SAMANTA

I AM SiXYears.OLD.

I loveCats,

I turned Seven.

①

I go to P.S. 3.   I am in the First Grade.

I go to PS3. I am in the First grade.

②

I have a hearing aid. I wear it in my

left ear.

I have a Hearing aid. I wear it in my left ear.

③

It helps me hear better because it makes the sounds louder.

It helps me hear better because it makes the sounds louder.

I use an FM unit with my hearing aid in school. This is the receiver. I call it a *'boot.'*

I use a FM
unit with my
hearing aid
in school.
This is the
receiver. I call
it a boot.

This is the FM transmitter. The teacher

wears the transmitter.

This is the
FM transmitter
The teacher
wears the
transmitter.

6

The teacher wears it around her neck. The mic should be no more than six inches from her mouth.

The teacher
wears it
around
her neck.
the mic should
be no more than
six inches
from her mouth ⑦

This is me wearing my *'boot'* and hearing aid.

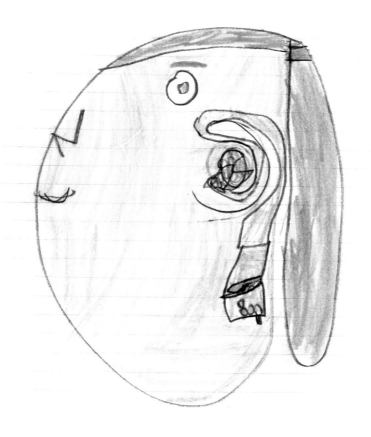

This is me
weanlig my
boot and hearing
aid.

The teacher needs to use the trans-

mitter when we have:

1. Story time

2. Classroom lesson

3. Explaining homework

4. Giving directions

The teacher needs to use
the transmitter when we haves
1. Story Time 2. Classroom lesson
3. Explaining homework
4 Giving Directions

This transmitter has different buttons. The top button turns it on. I look on the screen to see if it's on the right channel. My channel is N72. If it's not working, I press the *sync* button.

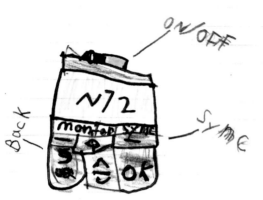

ON/OFF

SYNC

Back

∿72

monitor SYNC

this transmitter has
different buttons.
the top button
turns it on.
I look on the screen
to see if it's the
right channel. my
channel is N7a.
if it's not working
I press the -
Sync Button.

19

If it doesn't work, I take off my hearing aid. I open the battery door and then I close it. This turns on the FM unit.

If it doesn't work
I take off my
hearing aid.
I open the
battery door
and then I close
it this turns on the

Every afternoon when I'm leaving school I need to recharge my FM unit. I plug it into the charger.

Every afternoon when
I'm leaving school
I need to recharge
my FM. I plug it
in to the charger.

When I'm changing the battery of my hearing aid, I open the bottom of the hearing aid.

When I'm changing the battery of my hearing aid I open the bottom of the hearing aid

13

When I go to a different class, I tell the teacher I have an FM unit they should use.   If they don't know how to use it, I tell them what to do.

when I go to
a different class
I tell
the teacher
I have an FM
they should use
if they don't know
how to use it It
tell them what to do. ⑭

Now you know how to use a hearing aid and FM unit. Good luck with it. I like using it and so will you.

Now you know how to use a hearing aid and a FM. Good luck with it. I Like using it and So will you.

the End ⑮

Made in the USA
Middletown, DE
28 February 2018